Music Theory: Simple Music Theory for Electronic Music Production

Beginner's Guide to Rhythm, Chords, Scales, Modes, and a lot, lot more…

Roy Wilkenfeld

Copyright © 2015 Roy Wilkenfeld

All Rights Reserved

This is a work of fiction. Names, characters, places, and incidents are a product of the author's imagination. Any resemblance to actual persons, events, or locales is entirely coincidental.

This book or any portion thereof may not be reproduced or used in any manner whatsoever without the express written permission of the author except for the use of brief quotations in a book review.

The information provided in this book is meant to supplement, not replace, any proper training in the field of music.

All images used in this book are Royalty Free and/or fall under the Creative Commons license.

ISBN-13: 978-1534728905

ISBN-10: 1534728902

What Is This Book?

Music Theory: Simple Music Theory for Electronic Music Production is a beginner-friendly introductory guide to music theory, especially aimed for electronic music producers.

In this modern age, with the abundance of electronic music production platforms and software, music production has never been easier. Though it is easy to get into making music, music theory itself can be an intimidating topic both to beginners and seasoned producers.

This book aims to crush the intimidation-factor of music theory and bring back the joy into learning music – making music theory a fun, natural part of the music production process again.

With clear, inspiring images and easy-to-understand descriptions, the book encourages its readers to intuitive learning without getting lost in the jungle of frustrating music theory.

Music theory is fun and an essential tool to creating better music than ever – as it should be!

How to Use This Book

This book serves its purpose best as a guide while making actual music, always having it available on a desk nearby.

It is recommended to read through the book at least once, to spark inspiration in music, as well as new musical ideas and directions. After that, the book can be used as a tool and guidance to help overcome musical barriers during immersive music production sessions.

A MIDI keyboard or a piano is essential to get the most learning out of this book. As you tackle a new subject, inserting theory into practice instantly is the wisest choice. You'll visualize music theory better with a piano keyboard, always ready to try the things you have learned.

Music Theory is not only a great music production tool – it is a rich source of information about the basics of music theory. Learn musical terms and applications to make sure the information dives deep in your musical brain to create a routine from it – your music will thank you as will your constantly rising professional capabilities.

Contents

Introduction 1

Chapter 1 - The Basics 3

   01 The Piano Keyboard 3

   02 Intervals 6

   03 The Major Scale 9

   04 The Minor Scale 11

Chapter 2 – Modes of the Major Scale 13

   05 Dorian Mode 15

   06 Phrygian Mode 17

   07 Lydian Mode 18

   08 Mixolydian Mode 19

Chapter 3 – The Basics of Rhythm 21

   09 Tempo 21

   10 Bars and Time Signatures 23

   11 Rhythmic Note Values 25

Chapter 4 – The Harmonic Structure of Chords 28

12 Triads 28

13 Seventh Chords 31

14 Inversions of Triads 35

Chapter 5 – Melody and Transposition 39

15 Melody from Chords 39

16 Easy Transposition 42

Chapter 6 – List of Major and Minor Scales and Modes 45

17 Major Scales 45

18 Minor Scales 47

19 Modes 49

Conclusion 51

Introduction

Music Theory is divided into six chapters, all of them serving a unique purpose.

Chapter 1 includes the very basics and the essential knowledge, concentrating on the piano keyboard. The basics are very important knowledge, forming the pillars for the rest of the book.

Chapter 2 is all about modality – the modes of the major scale. Modes are often thought as the "spice" in music. Learn them and be surprised!

Chapter 3 introduces the rhythmic foundation for music, which is important in all music, but a critical element in electronic music.

Chapter 4 explains basic chords and their structures. For any songwriting and producing duties, it's very important to learn chords and how to play them.

Chapter 5 talks about melody and transposition, how to write a simple melody and how to "move" your music into a different key using transposition.

Chapter 6 includes clear tables and lists of all major and minor scales and modes, which can be easily used for reference whenever you're struggling with scales.

Have fun with music theory and don't be scared of it – because there's nothing to be scared of. When you start to understand the concepts of music theory, your music production confidence will gain a noticeable boost, for good.

I hope you get to learn a lot from this book, and I hope you get to have as much fun with it as I did while writing the book!

Thank you,

-Roy Wilkenfeld

Chapter 1 - The Basics

01 The Piano Keyboard

When it comes to learning notes and letters, intervals, whole- or semitones, sharps and flats, scales and chords, or music theory in general, the piano keyboard is the easiest way to understanding. Everything is easily visualized on the piano keyboard.

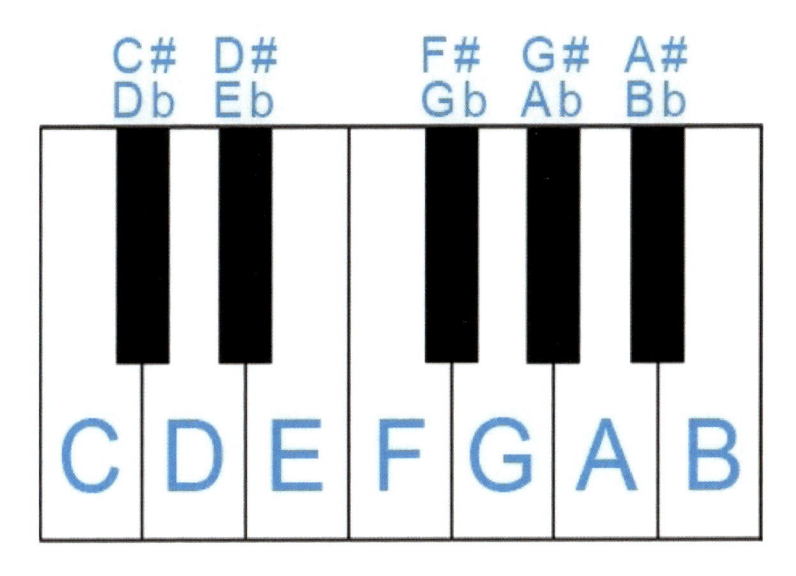

1 The keys on the piano and their musical names.

Chapter 1 The Basics

The image above represents the piano keyboard, including all 12 **pitches**. When going left on the piano keyboard, the sound decreases in pitch. Going right, the sound increases in pitch.

The white keys are called **natural tones** and the black keys are called **sharps (♯) and flats (♭)**. A sharp raises the pitch by a semitone, a flat lowers the pitch by a semitone. To avoid confusion, it's worth noting that a sharp and the corresponding flat are in fact the same key (e.g. C# and Db are both the same black key).

A **semitone** is the distance from a key to the next neighboring key. A **whole tone** is the distance of two semitones. The distance from C to C♯ is a semitone, while the distance from C to D is a whole tone.

An **interval** is the distance from any note to another note. For example, the distance between C and G is an interval. Intervals are discussed in detail in the next section.

Pro Tip #1: Real acoustic pianos normally have a total of 88 keys. MIDI keyboards are available in different sizes, such as 25, 37, 49 or 61 keys. To be able to play a wide area of pitches at once, just like a real piano, at least 37 keys are recommended. If you've got enough room in your studio, aim for as big keyboard as you can. The closer you are to a real piano, the better the whole learning and playing process will become.

Pro Tip #2: The piano keyboard works in the way of repeating a certain pattern of notes over and over again throughout the length of the keyboard. This pattern of notes is shown above. (C, D, E, F, G, A, B – then it starts from C again.)

Chapter 1 The Basics

02 INTERVALS

Intervals are the distance between two notes. Intervals have names and unique sounds to them each. Try playing each interval on your piano keyboard to learn their sound and character.

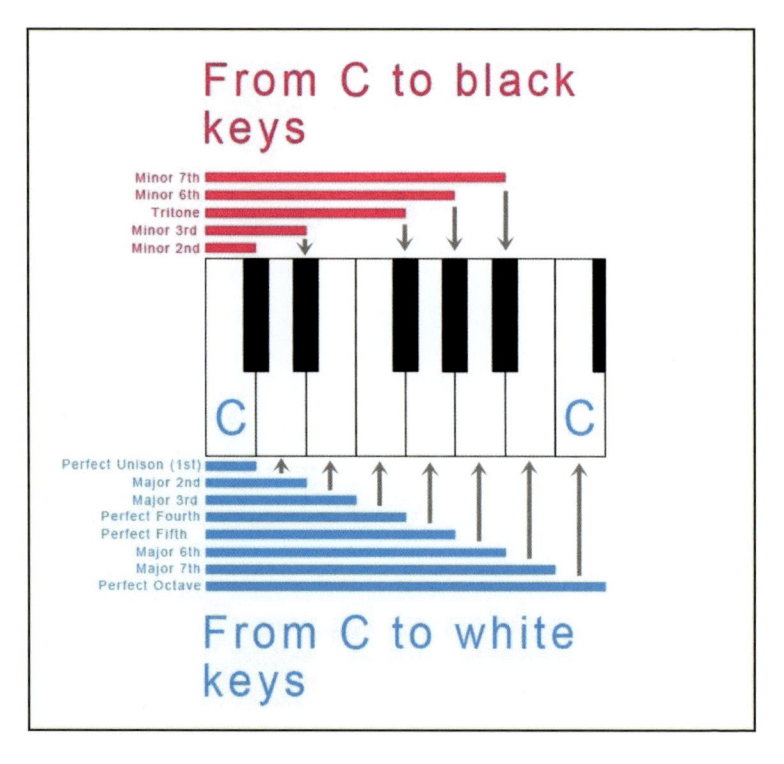

2 Intervals inside an octave's range.

A **perfect unison** means an exact pitch, just one note, technically not qualifying as an interval.

A **minor 2nd** is a one semitone interval, while a **major 2nd** spans a whole tone.

A **minor 3rd** is three semitones of length, and a **major 3rd** is four semitones, or two whole tones.

A **perfect fourth** spans five semitones

A **tritone** is a six semitone, or three whole tone, interval. Tritone is a special interval in the sense that it is the same distance from both directions of an octave. For instance, going up from C to F♯ is six semitones, as well as going down from C to F♯.

A **perfect fifth** spans seven semitones.

A **minor 6th** is eight semitones, or four whole tones, of length. A **major 6th** is nine semitones.

A **minor 7th** spans ten semitones, or five whole tones. A **major 7th** spans eleven semitones, acting as the final interval before an octave is reached.

A **perfect octave** is an interval where a certain note is played at a higher or lower pitch, spanning twelve semitones, or six whole tones. This interval is normally called just an **octave**.

Chapter 1 The Basics

Pro Tip: Practice intervals and their emotions in sound. You'll start to notice different intervals in music all around you, especially in melodies and harmonies. This is how you'll start to understand how to utilize different intervals better in your own music.

03 THE MAJOR SCALE

The major scale is the foundation of any other scale, as well as one of the most commonly used scales in music.

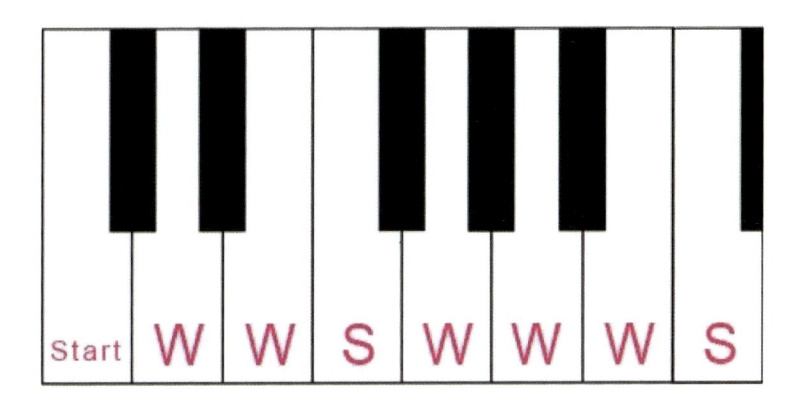

3 The major scale formula, with the C major scale as an example.

A **scale** is a set of notes dominated by a fundamental pitch. The C major scale emphasizes its fundamental pitch, C, which is also the starting point of the scale.

The **major scale** can easily be derived from a simple formula, consisting of whole tones (**W**) and semitones (**S**). The formula of a major scale is: *whole tone, whole tone, semitone, whole tone, whole tone, whole tone, semitone.*

The major scale is also known as the **Ionian mode**. The sound of the major scale could be described as "happy", "satisfied" or "successful".

Chapter 1 The Basics

Keep in mind that the scale formulas are universal, which means you can play any scale just by following the formula on the piano keyboard. For instance, you would get a D major scale by starting from the note D and applying the major scale formula, shown above.

You'll find all major scales listed [at the end of the book](#).

Pro Tip: As you play the scales, say the formula out loud as you press the notes on the piano keyboard, "start" being the first note to play: "Start, whole tone, whole tone, semitone, whole tone, whole tone, whole tone, semitone."

04 THE MINOR SCALE

The minor scale is another common scale in music. Together with the major scale, they form a musical basis for popular music.

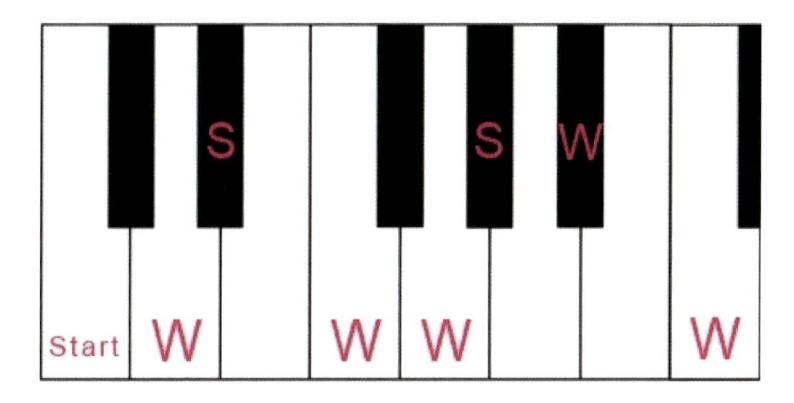

4 The minor scale formula, with the C minor scale as an example.

Just like the major scale, the **minor scale** also has a formula, which is: whole tone, semitone, whole tone, whole tone, semitone, whole tone, whole tone.

The minor scale is also known as the **Aeolian mode**. The sound of the minor scale could be described as "melancholic", "emotional" or even "sad".

Modes are further discussed in Chapter 2.

You'll find all minor scales listed at the end of the book.

Chapter 1 The Basics

Pro Tip: Play the C minor scale and the C major scale back-to-back, to learn how they differ on the piano keyboard.

Chapter 2 – Modes of the Major Scale

Modes in music are easy to understand when they are thought as **alterations** of the major scale. The minor scale, discussed earlier, is the sixth mode of the major scale, therefore an alteration of the first mode, the major scale itself.

The great thing about modes is, they all have a certain *feel* to them, which is a great tool in songwriting. Modes are also very easy to understand, if you don't let yourself feel intimidated by them.

The major scale is the same as Ionian mode, and the minor scale equals to Aeolian mode. Here is a list of all modern western modes.

1. Ionian
2. Dorian
3. Phrygian
4. Lydian
5. Mixolydian
6. Aeolian

Note: There is a seventh mode, the Locrian mode, which is not included in the list to avoid confusion. Simply put, the Locrian mode is virtually never used in music.

Additionally, you'll find all modes listed *at the end of the book*, including their notes.

05 Dorian Mode

The Dorian mode is the second mode of the major scale.

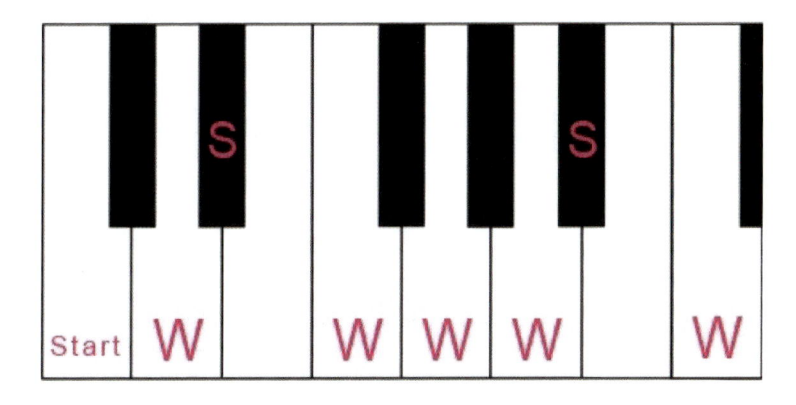

5 The Dorian mode formula, with C Dorian as an example.

The Dorian mode is almost the same as the minor scale, but it includes a major 6th note, instead of a minor 6th.

The Dorian mode could be described as "dreamy" or "misty", and it's not quite happy or sad either – more like something in between.

The formula for the Dorian mode goes as follows: whole tone, semitone, whole tone, whole tone, whole tone, semitone, whole tone.

Chapter 2 Modes of the Major Scale

Pro Tip: When figuring out the Dorian mode, think about playing a regular minor scale, but make sure to change the minor 6th interval of the scale to a major 6th.

06 PHRYGIAN MODE

The Phrygian mode is the third mode of the major scale.

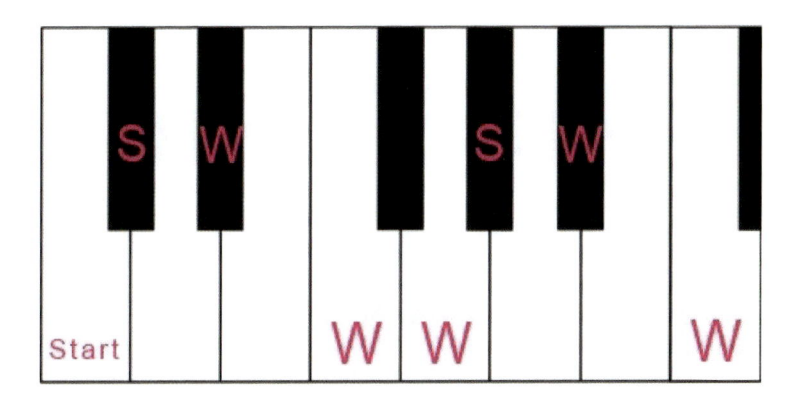

6 The Phrygian mode formula, with C Phrygian as an example.

The Phrygian mode is similar to the minor scale, but it has a minor 2nd instead of a major 2nd.

The feeling of the Phrygian mode can be described as "dark" and "powerful".

The formula for the Phrygian mode is: semitone, whole tone, whole tone, whole tone, semitone, whole tone, whole tone.

Pro Tip: When practicing the Phrygian mode, think about playing the minor scale, only with a minor 2nd instead of a major 2nd.

Chapter 2 Modes of the Major Scale

07 Lydian Mode

The Lydian mode is the fourth mode of the major scale.

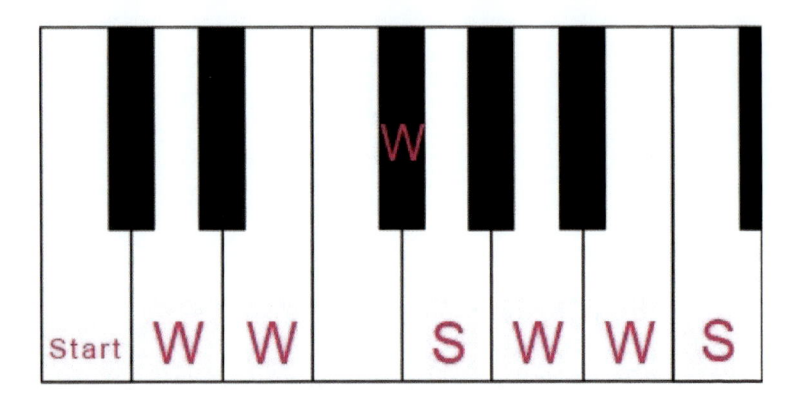

7 The Lydian mode formula, with C Lydian as an example.

The Lydian mode differs from the major scale by having a sharpened fourth. In C Lydian, the 4th note is F# instead of F, as in the regular major scale.

The Lydian mode can be described as "energetic" and "bright".

The formula for the Lydian mode goes as follows: whole tone, whole tone, whole tone, semitone, whole tone, whole tone, semitone.

Pro Tip: When practicing the Lydian mode, just think about playing the major scale but sharpening the 4th note.

08 Mixolydian Mode

The Mixolydian mode is the fifth mode of the major scale.

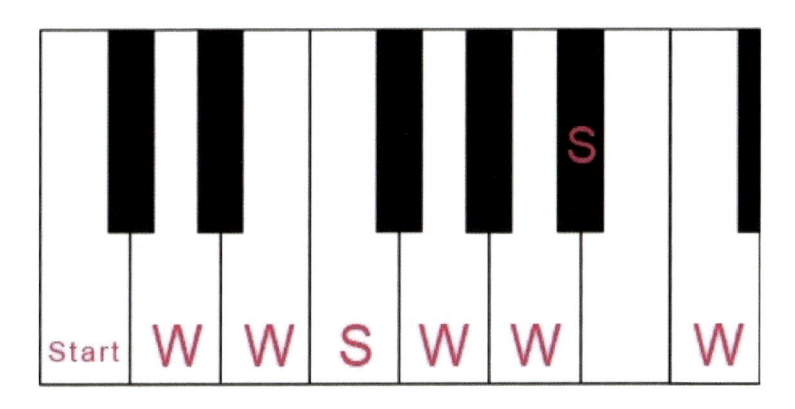

8 The Mixolydian mode formula, with C Mixolydian as an example.

The Mixolydian mode differs from the major scale by having a minor 7th instead of a major 7th. In C Mixolydian, the 7th note is Bb instead of C major's B.

The Mixolydian mode has a somewhat similar sound to the Dorian mode, though it is a bit brighter. The Mixolydian mode could be described as "spirited" or "cloudy".

The formula for the Mixolydian mode is: whole tone, whole tone, semitone, whole tone, whole tone, semitone, whole tone.

Chapter 2 Modes of the Major Scale

Pro Tip: When practicing the Mixolydian mode, think of it as the major scale, only with a minor 7th instead of a major 7th.

Chapter 3 – The Basics of Rhythm

09 Tempo

Tempo equals to speed in music.

125 BPM

9 Tempo is usually showed in BPM, or beats-per-minute.

Some music is slower and some faster. The speed of music is dictated by the **tempo**. Tempo is usually calculated by beats-per-minute, or **BPM**. To electronic music producers, the concept of BPM is a familiar one, as the tempo of the project needs to be set in a digital audio workstation when starting the music production process.

A **beat** is an event that repeats regularly over time, a *pulse*. At the BPM of 125, the speed of the music would be 125 beats-per-minute. In electronic dance music, the beat is usually the kick drum. Try tapping your fingers to a piece of music and you'll better understand the concept of beat.

Chapter 3 The Basics of Rhythm

Pro Tip: To find out the tempo of your favorite music, use the "tap to tempo" –function in your DAW to calculate the approximate tempo in real time, tapping as the music plays. Consult the manual of your DAW for more information on how the function works.

10 BARS AND TIME SIGNATURES

On the macro level, music consists of a time signature, following bars, which enable the building of a piece of music.

In music, a **bar** (or **measure**) is a division of time, which includes a number of beats. Bars separate music into "building blocks", which makes the process of following and creating music easier.

A **time signature** dictates how many beats are in a bar. In addition, a time signature also tells which note values equal to beats.

Chapter 3 The Basics of Rhythm

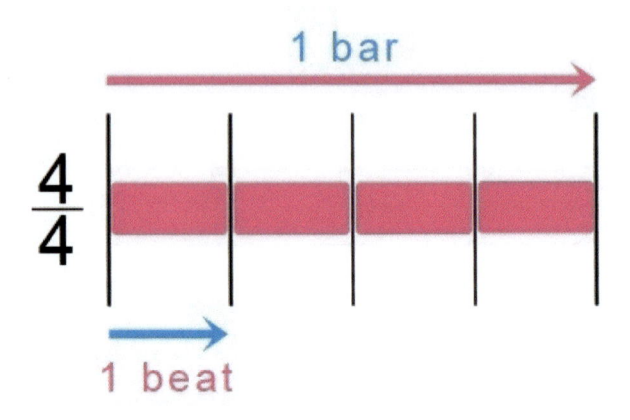

10 The illustration of one bar in 4/4 time signature.

The picture above shows one bar filled with four beats, dictated by a 4/4 time signature. In the time signature number, the **number above the line** represents the amount of beats in a bar. The **number below the line** reveals which note value equals to one beat. In this example, the note value is a quarter note (more about note values in the next section).

As an easy reminder, the majority of electronic dance music and popular music are in the easy-to-follow 4/4 time signature.

Pro Tip: Other common (and not-so-common) time signatures are: 6/8, 3/8, 2/2, ¾ and 5/4. Experiment with time signatures to give your music a special twist!

11 RHYTHMIC NOTE VALUES

Music consists of notes of different lengths. Especially drum patterns serve as great examples of rhythmic notes.

Whole notes (1/1) are the same length as one bar.

Half notes (1/2) are half-a-bar of length.

Four **quarter notes** (1/4) are included in a bar.

When quarter notes are divided in half, **eight notes** (1/8) are born.

When eight notes are split, you get **sixteenth notes** (1/16).

Chapter 3 The Basics of Rhythm

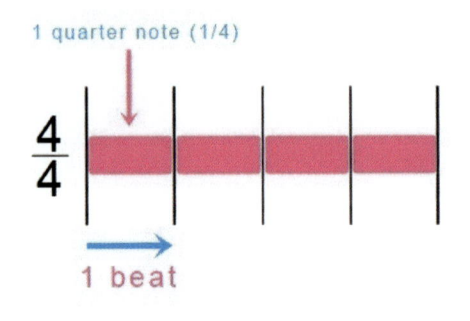

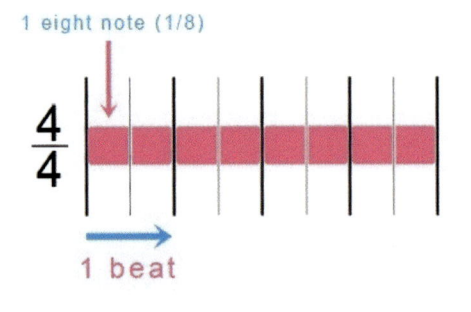

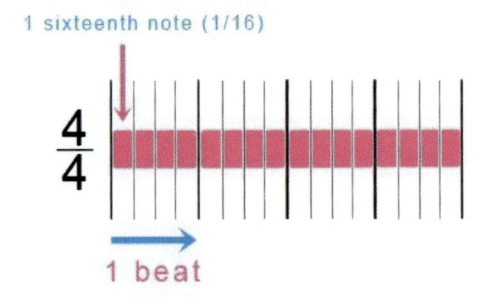

11 Quarter, eight and sixteenth notes in a bar.

The image above illustrates the further division of the quarter note. For creating a proper electronic groove, eight and sixteenth notes are essential to building full-sounding, driving rhythms.

Pro Tip: Note values can get really small, from 1/32, 1/64 to 1/128 and so on. Be reasonable though, as 1/32 or 1/64 notes are usually the smallest note values needed when constructing music or a drum groove.

Chapter 3 The Basics of Rhythm

Chapter 4 – The Harmonic Structure of Chords

12 Triads

Triads are basic chords in which three notes are played at the same time.

A **triad** chord contains three notes: **root** (1st), third (3rd) and fifth (5th) notes. These notes in a chord are called **chord tones**. Reference the intervals in chapter 2 in case of confusion.

The first note is called a root so the chord can be easily identified. For example, in a C major triad, the root is C. The term "root" is only used when talking about chords.

Triads can be major or minor, depending on whether the chord includes a major or minor 3rd interval.

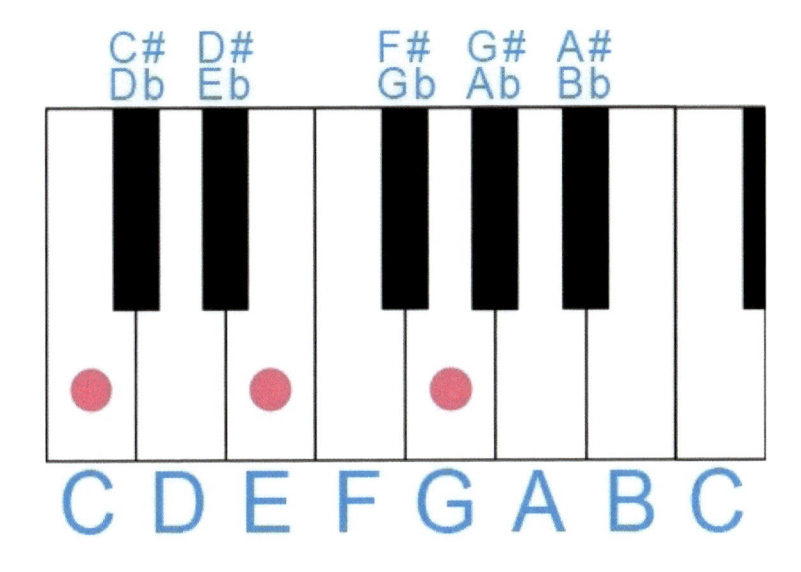

12 C major triad.

In the image above, a C **major triad** is illustrated. The notes included are: C (the root), E (major 3rd) and G (fifth).

Chapter 4 The Harmonic Structure of Chords

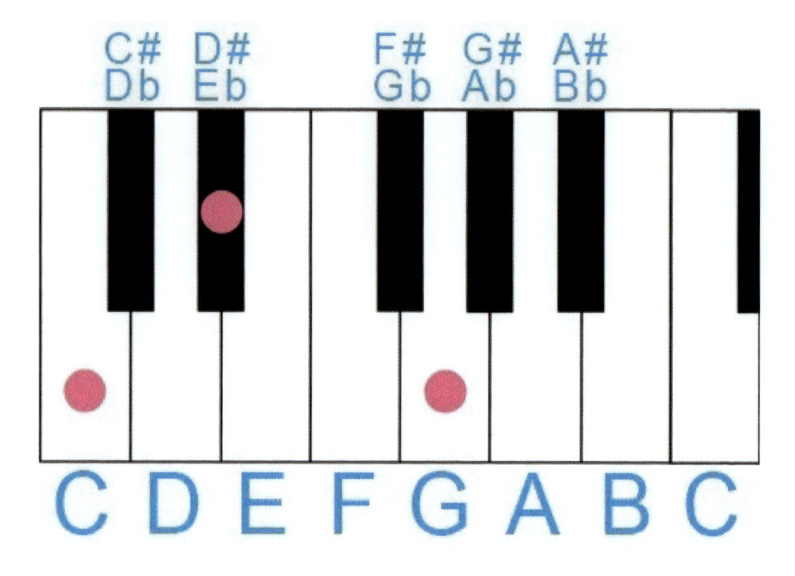

13 C minor triad.

In the image above, a C **minor triad** is illustrated, including C (the root), Eb (minor 3rd) and G (fifth).

Pro Tip: Use triads to get a harmonic structure for a song quickly. Triads are the easiest of chords which makes them ideal for quick songwriting purposes and sketching down a chordal idea.

13 Seventh Chords

Seventh chords are like triads, but with a seventh note on top.

Seventh chords are constructed from the root (1st), third (3rd) and fifth (5th) and seventh (7th) notes. Seventh chords are richer-sounding chords than triads, due to the seventh note, giving them a "smoother" and even a "jazzy" nature.

There are a few different kinds of seventh chords, which can be used in music, the most popular of which are the major seventh, minor seventh and dominant seventh chords.

Again, reference the intervals in chapter 2 to remind you of the intervals used in forming chords.

Chapter 4 The Harmonic Structure of Chords

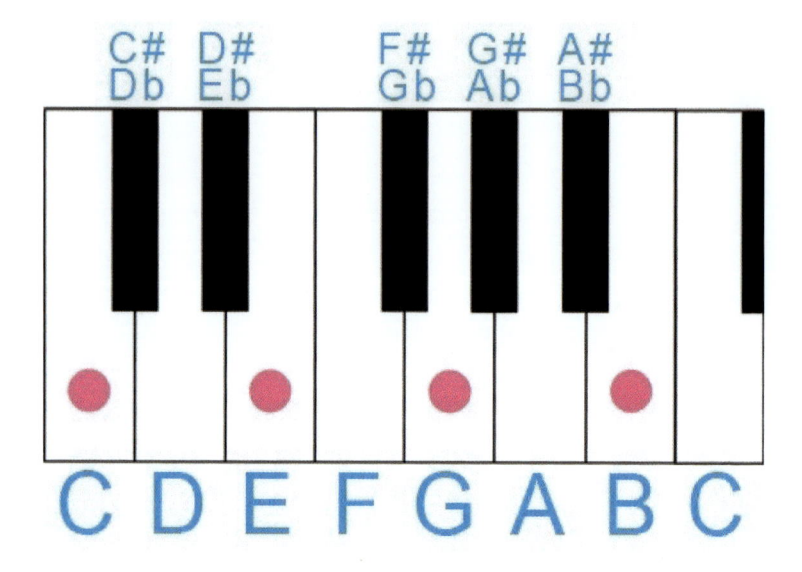

14 C major seventh chord.

The image above shows a C **major seventh chord**, with C (root), E (major 3rd), G (5th) and B (major 7th). If a seventh chord has a major 3rd and a major 7th, it is a major seventh chord.

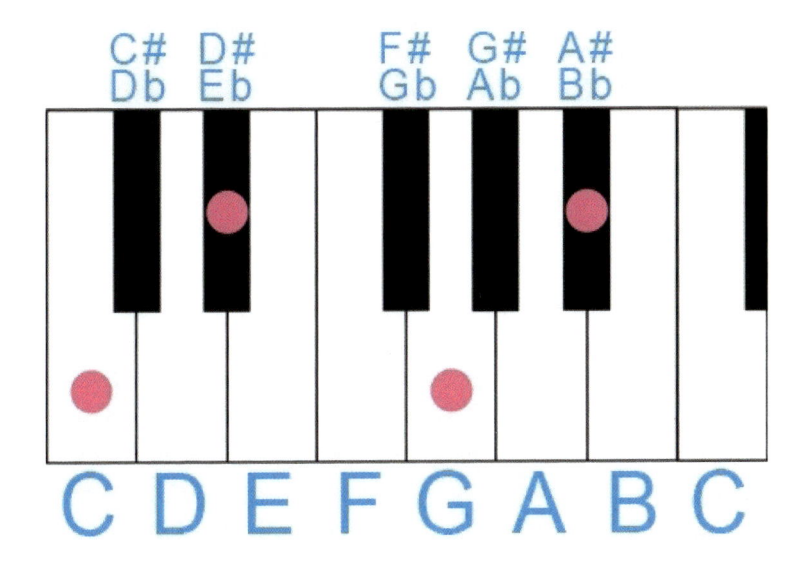

15 C minor seventh chord.

The image above shows a C **minor seventh chord**, with C (root), Eb (minor 3rd), G (5th) and Bb (minor 7th). If a seventh chord has a minor 3rd and a minor 7th, it is a minor seventh chord.

Chapter 4 The Harmonic Structure of Chords

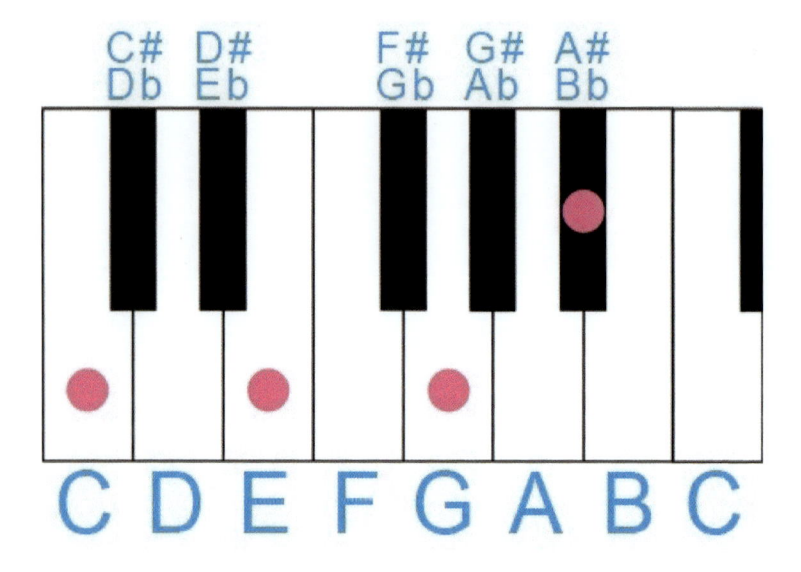

16 C dominant seventh chord.

The image above shows a C **dominant seventh chord**, with C (root), E (major 3rd), G (5th) and B (minor 7th). If a seventh chord has a major 3rd but a minor 7th, it is a **dominant seventh chord**.

Pro Tip #1: If you want to make jazzy-sounding house music for example, use major 7th chords to provide that smooth feeling. Use minor 7th chords if you want to energize your minor triads.

Pro Tip #2: Dominant 7ths provide a very tense feeling to the music. They are best used when wanting to suggest a change of chord in a chord progression. For example: C dominant 7th followed by a D minor triad. Try it and see what happens!

14 INVERSIONS OF TRIADS

Triads can be inverted to create a different flavor of the same chord.

A chord inversion happens in a triad when the 3rd or 5th note acts as the **bass note** (the lowest note in the chord) instead of the root.

For example, a regular C major triad can be inverted by transferring the C note to the top of the chord, leaving E act as the bass note. This is called the **first inversion**.

From the first inversion position, if the lowest note E is transferred on top of the chord, leaving G to act as the bass note, we get the **second inversion**.

Chapter 4 The Harmonic Structure of Chords

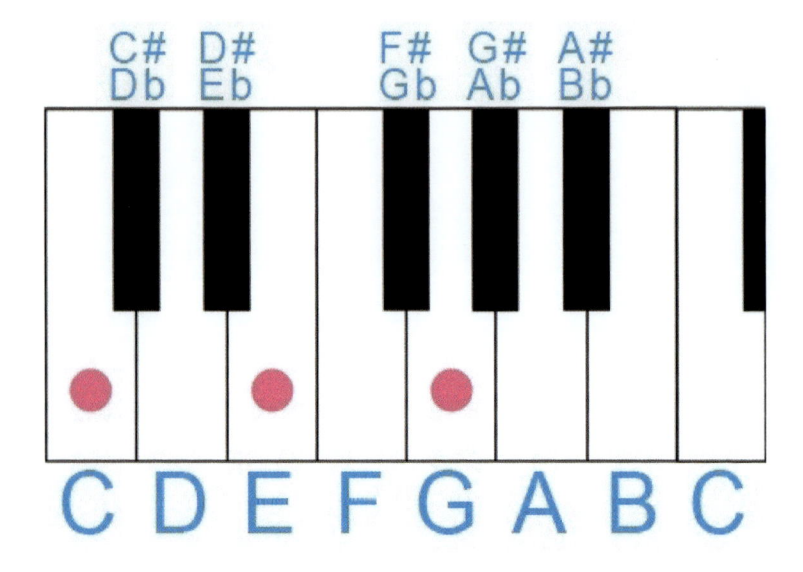

17 C major triad, no inversion.

The image above shows the basic C major triad, no inversion applied. Use this to compare to the following images where inversions are applied.

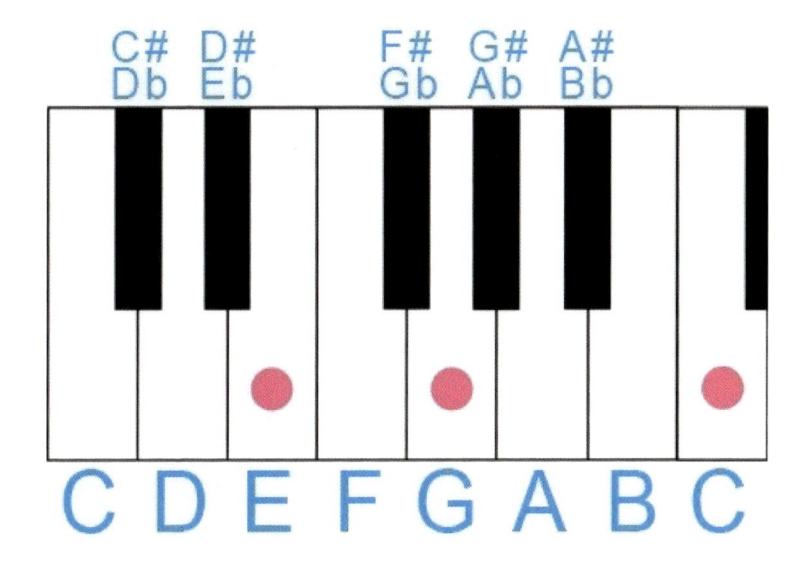

18 C major triad, first inversion.

The image above shows the first inversion of a C major triad. Notice the C has been transferred from the bottom to the top.

Chapter 4 The Harmonic Structure of Chords

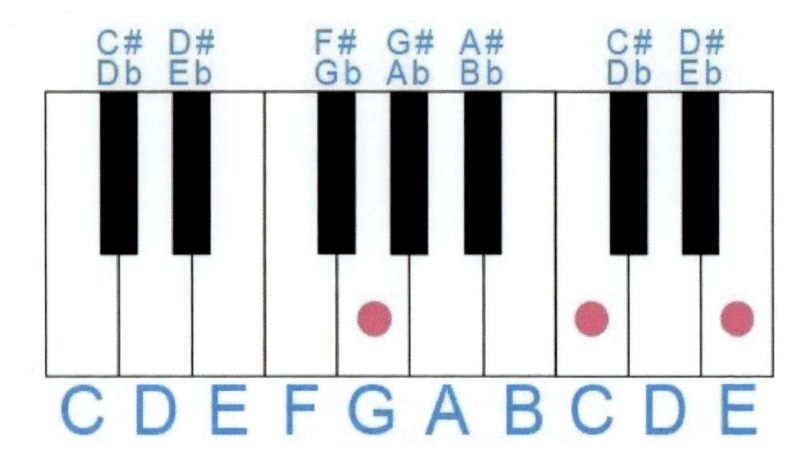

19 C major triad, second inversion.

The image above shows the second inversion of a C major triad. Notice, this is a continuation of the first inversion, taking the E from the bottom to the top.

As you might have guessed, should one more inversion be applied, the result would be a basic C major triad, making a full circle back to the starting position!

Pro Tip: Take advantage of inversions to find the right sounding chord when making a track. Sometimes one inversion might sound better than the other, giving you a small palette of choice.

Chapter 5 – Melody and Transposition

15 Melody from Chords

Chords can be taken further by extracting melodies from them.

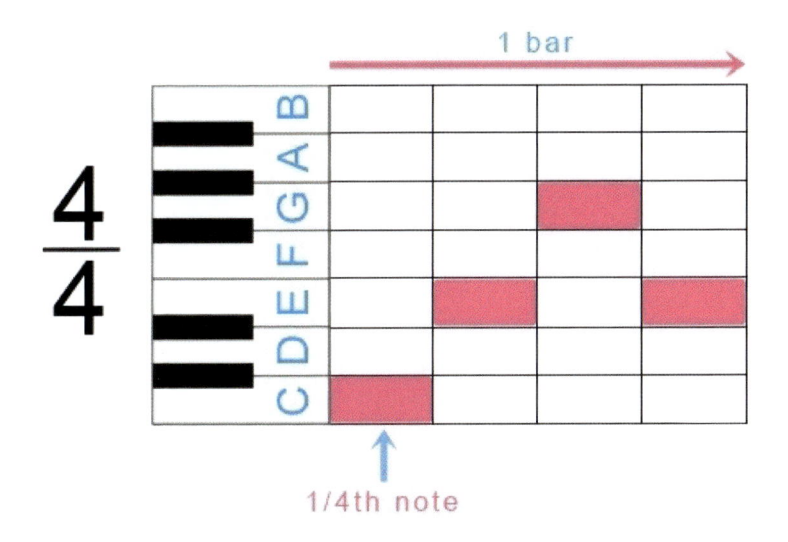

20 A simple melody from a C major chord.

In the image above, a C major triad has been transformed into a simple melody by utilizing quarter notes and playing the chord tones.

Chapter 5 Melody and Transposition

Any chord can be broken down into an interesting melody, by playing the chord tones with different note values, such as quarter, eight and sixteenth notes, or any mixture of them.

Melodies created from chords are also known as **arpeggios**.

Pro Tip #1: If you use a synthesizer, fire up the arpeggiator in it to create automatic melodic sequences. Simply play a chord and the synthesizer will do the rest.

Pro Tip #2: Arpeggios are a great songwriting tool where movement is wanted instead of a static chord.

Chapter 5 Melody and Transposition

16 Easy Transposition

Transposition in music means changing the musical key.

Any note, chord or melody can be **transposed** to a different musical **key**. For example, a piece of music written in the key of C major can be transposed to D major instead. A key simply means a group of notes in a scale – the pattern of notes a song is made of.

To transpose a whole song into a new key, all musical notes have to be moved **chromatically** to the desired key, meaning every note moves the same amount. Let's look at an illustration to make the process simpler.

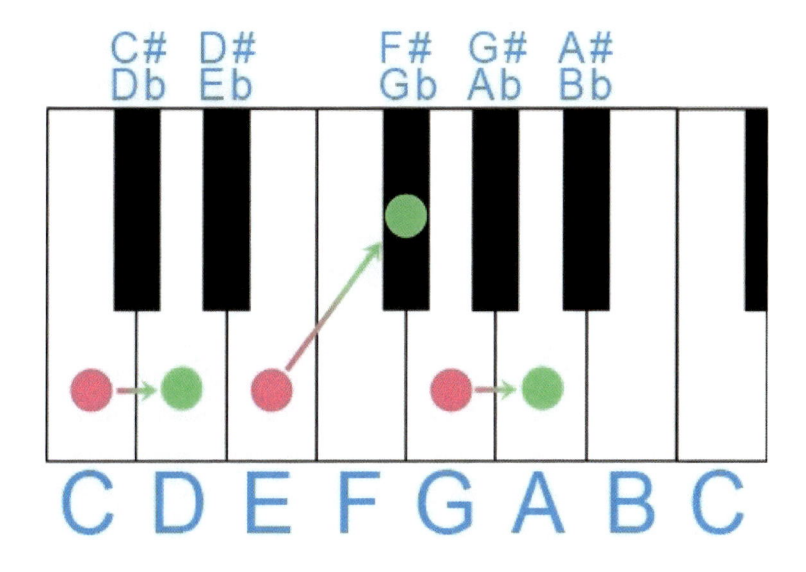

21 C major triad transposed to D major.

The image above displays the process of transposition. C major triad (in pink) is transposed to a D major triad (in green). All notes move two semitones, maintaining their relative positions.

Chapter 5 Melody and Transposition

In brief, any major key can be transposed to any other major key, and any minor key can be transposed to any other minor key.

Practice tip: Start from C and transpose a C major chord to every other major triad, and do the same with minor triads – you'll get the feeling of how triads are formed on the piano keyboard and memorize them.

Pro Tip #1: Transposition is a great tool in songwriting. For example, you could write a song in the key of C, and transpose it later to another key. The advantage of transposing like this is to find a suitable "vibe" to the music, by trying out other keys. Of course, for this kind of transposition to work properly, you'd have to use MIDI notes in your digital audio workstation to easily transpose them.

Pro Tip #2: Another great use for transposition is when working with a vocalist. All vocalists have their key ranges in singing. For example, if the track you made causes problems for the vocalist to sing properly, you can easily transpose it to a comfortable key for the vocalist, to sing at the correct pitch for their voice.

Chapter 6 – List of Major and Minor Scales and Modes

17 Major Scales

Every major scale is listed below, for learning and practice purposes.

Use the table below to practice all major scales on the piano keyboard, together with the numbered intervals.

You might wonder why some scales are written in flats instead of sharps, and the answer is simplicity. The important thing to remember is that the scales are **exactly the same** in sound, they only look different on paper (e.g. C# / Db major).

Scale	1st	2nd	3rd	4th	5th	6th	7th	
C major	C	D	E	F	G	A	B	C
C# / Db major	Db	Eb	F	Gb	Ab	Bb	C	Db
D major	D	E	F#	G	A	B	C#	D
D# / Eb major	Eb	F	G	Ab	Bb	C	D	Eb
E major	E	F#	G#	A	B	C#	D#	E
F major	F	G	A	Bb	C	D	E	F
F# / Gb major	Gb	Ab	Bb	Cb	Db	Eb	F	Gb
G major	G	A	B	C	D	E	F#	G
G# / Ab major	Ab	Bb	C	Db	Eb	F	G	Ab
A major	A	B	C#	D	E	F#	G#	A
A# / Bb major	Bb	C	D	Eb	F	G	A	Bb
B major	B	C#	D#	E	F#	G#	A#	B

Pro Tip: By looking at the table, you can easily form every major triad and seventh chord from any major scale. The root, 3rd, 5th and 7th notes are colored in blue.

18 Minor Scales

Every minor scale is listed below.

Use the table below to practice all minor scales on the piano keyboard, together with the numbered intervals.

Scale	1st	2nd	3rd	4th	5th	6th	7th	
C minor	C	D	Eb	F	G	Ab	Bb	C
C# / Db minor	C#	D#	E	F#	G#	A	B	C#
D minor	D	E	F	G	A	Bb	C	D
D# / Eb minor	Eb	F	Gb	Ab	Bb	Cb	Db	Eb
E minor	E	F#	G	A	B	C	D	E
F minor	F	G	Ab	Bb	C	Db	Eb	F
F# / Gb minor	F#	G#	A	B	C#	D	E	F#
G minor	G	A	Bb	C	D	Eb	F	G
G# / Ab minor	G#	A#	B	C#	D#	E	F#	G#
A minor	A	B	C	D	E	F	G	A
A# / Bb minor	Bb	C	Db	Eb	F	Gb	Ab	Bb
B minor	B	C#	D	E	F#	G	A	B

Chapter 6 List of Major and Minor Scales and Modes

Pro Tip #1: You might have noticed that A minor indeed has all the same notes as C major. That's right. A minor is the **relative minor** of C major. You can calculate any major scale's relative minor scale by stepping down three semitones from the major scale's 1st note. For example, the relative minor of G major is E minor – they use all the same notes. The distance from G to E is three semitones downwards.

Pro Tip #2: Form every minor triad and seventh chord by using the table. The root, 3rd, 5th and 7th notes are colored in red.

19 MODES

In the table below, all modes are listed as they naturally appear on the piano keyboard's white keys.

The white keys of the piano include all modes. The white keys of the piano are designed to include the modal intervals without needing to use any sharps or flats, which makes playing the modal scales easy.

The distinctive "modal note" is highlighted in purple for Dorian, Phrygian, Lydian and Mixolydian modes.

Remember, Lydian and Mixolydian are variations of the major scale, whereas Dorian and Phrygian are variations of the minor scale – this is how they're memorized easily.

Mode	1st	2nd	3rd	4th	5th	6th	7th	
C Ionian (Major)	C	D	E	F	G	A	B	C
D Dorian	D	E	F	G	A	B	C	D
E Phrygian	E	F	G	A	B	C	D	E
F Lydian	F	G	A	B	C	D	E	F
G Mixolydian	G	A	B	C	D	E	F	G
A Aeolian (Minor)	A	B	C	D	E	F	G	A

Chapter 6 List of Major and Minor Scales and Modes

The table above shows all modes, immediately playable using the white keys only. Of course, should you want to form, for example, an E Dorian scale, you'll need to take a look at the mode formulas [in chapter 2](#) as you can't use only the white keys for that.

Pro Tip: The white keys of the piano are extremely useful in songwriting. Let's say you want to write a song in Dorian mode. Well, that's easy. Just use D as the bass note and play the rest of the white keys – it's impossible to miss a note.

CONCLUSION

That's all folks! Now take what you've learned and apply it in your music – I promise your music will get only better with the assistance of music theory. But always remember, no amount of music theory will write songs for you – they always come from your heart. ;)

Hey, I hope you enjoyed this book. Check out my other books to support you in making music and stay on top of your music production game...

-Roy Wilkenfeld

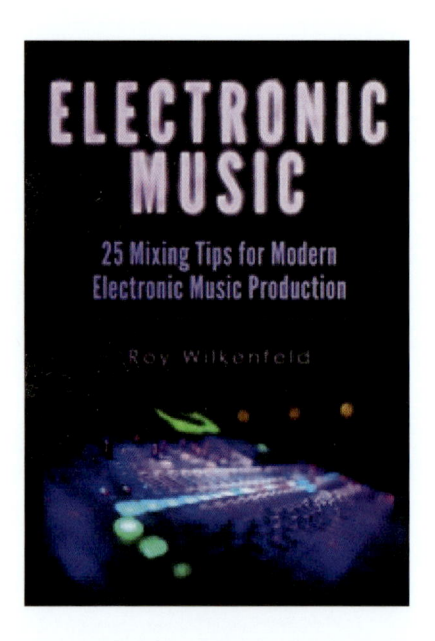

Electronic Music: 25 Mixing Tips for Modern Electronic Music Production

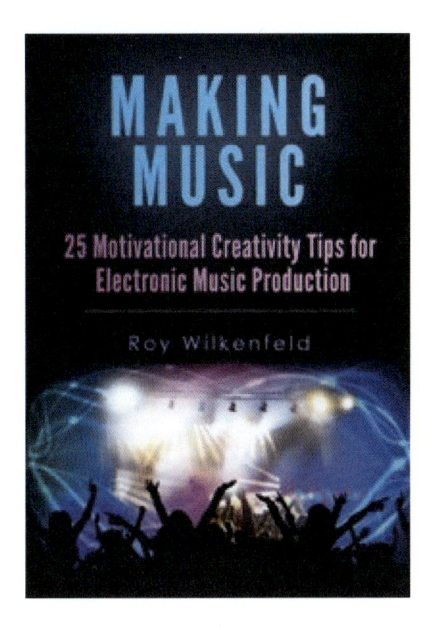

Making Music: 25 Motivational Creativity Tips for Electronic Music Production

THANK YOU FOR READING THIS BOOK

Please check out the Production Wisdom blog for more great tips and information about mixing, music production, techniques and philosophy.

productionwisdom.com

Printed in Great Britain
by Amazon